A Guidebook to Acquiring Food, Stockpiling, Storing, and Preparing for Survival

Creating Your Own Long-Term Cheap Storage Pantry and Cooking Lifesaving Supply Food for Self-Sufficiency in an Emergency. Survival Food List and Recipes

Geoffrey Richards

<u>Leave a review about our book:</u>

As an independent author with a small marketing budget, reviews are my livelihood on this platform. If you enjoyed this book, I'd really appreciate it, if you left your honest feedback. You can do so by clicking review button.
I love hearing my readers and I personally read every single review!

• • •

Table of Contents

Introduction

Unfortunately, food shortages are still quite rampant all around the world. The reasons vary for different people. Some are experiencing food shortages because of low production; others due to disasters, wars, or their country's poor economic conditions. No matter what the reasons may be, it is something that the world has been struggling with, and it will remain a vivid reality of human society.

The only thing we can do is be prepared and store food whenever we can.

This guide to food acquiring, storing, and stockpiling is written with the purpose of providing all the relevant information that you can use to store a large amount of food at home for your family.

Food storage requires a whole different level of understanding—from knowing the shelf lives of different food items to analyzing their utility, every detail demands attention. And if you're able to successfully get through this complicated process of stockpiling and storage, you can ensure food security for you and your family members for months to come.

So, if you wish to acquire some sense of food security, then give this book a read and take notes of all the important processes involved.

Chapter 1:
Why You Need a Food Storage Pantry

The importance of survival food storage cannot be neglected. No one can survive without a constant supply of food. Living without food and water causes malnutrition, deficiency diseases, and ultimately death. There are certain crisis conditions in which securing a regular supply of food is just not possible. The year 2020 is a recent example of such a crisis. Worldwide lockdowns made it difficult to go out and buy groceries on a weekly basis. Similarly, in other pandemics, war-like conditions, famine, and natural disasters, mankind is met the most difficult circumstances, and such conditions call for food stock that is available at home. This stock must be sufficient enough to meet the needs of every family member as well as ensure good health.

In this chapter, we will examine factors that make survival food important. We will learn how haphazard food management results in wasted resources, including the time and effort you put in. According to food science, only a well-planned and well-written food management program can guarantee good health and food security for a longer duration.

Following are some of the known benefits of survival food and its storage.

Survival During Crisis

Who knows how long a crisis will last? It can take weeks to months, depending on the changing circumstances. You cannot simply rely on external food sources in such changing and ever-wavering conditions. Running out of food and living for days without it is simply not a choice. The only argument that highlights the importance of survival food the most is that our existence depends on it. Now, imagine there is an impending crisis, and you are haphazardly stocking food in your house, and then the food supply is cut off. In a week or two, you will realize that you are running out of some of the basic ingredients needed to cook a complete meal. If only you had prepared a comprehensive list of items along with their required amounts, and then grocery shopped accordingly, such a situation could have been avoided!

Survival is more than living: It is about living a healthy and active life. For such a life, you must have everything healthy to eat. Without sufficient survival food stock at home, you cannot guarantee sound mental and physical health.

Food Security in Difficult Times

One of the profound reasons that we need to stock survival food at home is food security. It does not even have to be a crisis in order for us to do so. You can stock these items to have long-term food security as well. For instance, if you are always working and don't get enough time to consistently buy your groceries, having non-perishable survival food items stocked in your pantry will help big time.

Storing food for a month or more is commonplace in circumstances where there is a constant threat of food shortages or inflation. People then bulk buy the required items and store them in their pantries. Basement storage is also a common practice in places where there are harsh living conditions. People in those places keep their basements filled with survival food items for three to six months, or even for a year. For instance, people living in extremely cold climates stock up on food before winter.

Learning Food Management

The best part about survival food storage is that it equips you with all the right skills to manage food. Even on normal days, when we grocery shop and stock our kitchen cabinets with weekly staples, we tend to waste a lot of our energy, time, effort, and money due to our inadequate understanding of food and lack of management skills. But once you go through this whole process of survival food storage, from initial research to list-making, buying in bulk, obtaining appropriate storage items and materials, then packing the food and storing it in an orderly fashion, you become an expert at managing a large amount of food. And not only that, when you live on the survival food, you also learn how to effectively utilize that food without wasting a single bit of it. In order to increase the utility of the food, you also improve your cooking skills so that you can enjoy a variety of flavors and aromas.

Having these food management and utilization skills can prove to be more helpful on normal days. Now you will be able to buy more food on a smaller budget, and that food will be healthy and nutritious, carefully managed, and stored.

Uninterrupted Supply of Energy

The concept of survival food revolves around the provision of an adequate amount of energy to the body. In testing times, this food proves to be a constant source of energy for both the mind and the body. The list of the survival food shared in the next chapter rightly indicates that it consists of all those items that are a direct source of carbohydrates, proteins, and fats. The survival food storage techniques further teach how to best use this food to extract an adequate amount of energy per day to meet all the body's needs.

Help and Rescue

Once the survival food is stocked and packaged in suitable boxes and containers, it gets easier to take with you at the time of need, especially when you cannot leave with all your household items. A survival food package for three to four weeks must be kept ready separately so that you can take it anywhere in difficult circumstances. Whether you are hitchhiking or forest camping, this survival food can help sustain you for days without any fear.

Chapter 2
All About Your Perfect Pantry

Before you start hoarding and stocking food items at home, it is imperative to clearly see the survival food and what it should be like. Understanding the food you eat and how it stays fresh is the basic science that every prepper must learn in order to manage food over a long period of time. Only this understanding can help you use this food up to its best utility in a crisis. By examining the food's purpose, we can draw a complete picture of what we are looking for. There are certain features that every survival food must have. The following are some well-known features of survival food, which can be taken as a standard selection criterion to pick and choose food for long-term storage.

Storage-Friendly

What does it mean for food to be storage-friendly, a prepper may ask? Well, the food we are planning to consume must have all the features that would make this storage easier. It should be treated, managed, and stored properly. It must be light and portable to easily move it around in your pantry and use it whenever needed. Once this food is stored in a plastic bucket, PETE bottles, or other storage pouches, it should take up minimum space so you can store a large amount of food in a smaller space.

For instance, freeze-dried and dehydrated food items are suitable for longer-term storage, but freeze-dried food takes much bigger storage space than dehydrated food. So, the best choice is to store the bulk of dehydrated food instead of freeze-dried food. Dehydrated food can be considered more storage-friendly than freeze-dried food. Such subtle differences can make the food either suitable for storage or non-suitable for longer-term storage. Remember, the whole process should be kept as easy and convenient for you (as the prepper) as possible. You don't need to menu-fatigue yourself during the process.

Shelf Life

The next important criterion to choosing food for your survival storage is shelf life. It is that time period in which food or any other commodity can be kept or stored without the product losing its original quality and composition. When it comes to food, the shelf life indicates for how long the food is suitable for consumption; beyond the stated shelf life of the food, it can go bad, lose its nutritional value, or turn toxic. Many characteristics determine a food product's shelf life—for example, the content of the food, its sustainability, processing, packaging, and conditions of storage.

Expiration Dates

We commonly find expiration dates written on the food packaging, but the shelf life is hardly ever mentioned. It is because of the fact that both durations have different significance. The expiration date has importance from the manufacturer's standpoint, whereas shelf life is considered important when the same food is stored. The expiration date is mentioned to mark a time period in which that food must be consumed, and it is determined according to the ingredients and composition of the product, whereas shelf life determines the time period in which food remains to be fit for use. For example, even if pasteurized milk is marked with an expiration date of two weeks, the milk can go bad in just one day once it is opened and placed at room temperature; this means the milk does not have a longer shelf life.

Certain factors determine the shelf life of food, and by controlling these factors, we can extend that amount of time.

Non-Perishable Food Items

Before marking the survival food as non-perishable, it is important to learn the difference between perishable and non-perishable food. The classification is based on the food's quality to stay fresh. Perishable food items cannot stay fresh for more than a few hours at room temperature, and they can only sustain in low controlled temperatures such as refrigerators and freezers. Even in freezers and refrigerators, such items can only remain fresh for about two or three weeks, depending on their type and composition. For this reason, perishable food is not suitable for survival food storage. You can only store some for immediate and short-term use. Perishable food includes meat, fresh vegetables, fruits, dairy products (such as milk), and cooked food.

However, food classified as non-perishable can stay fresh and edible for longer durations. These food items do not go bad at room temperature, and they can be cooked easily for a complete meal. Flours, grains, legumes, pasta, whole and powdered spices, etc., are naturally non-perishable. There are some perishable products that can be converted into non-perishable ones through food processing. For instance, fruits like grapes that are otherwise perishable are dehydrated to make raisins that are non-perishable. Similarly, other methods can be employed to expand the fold of non-perishable food items and store them for long durations.

Cost-Effective

This characteristic of survival storage food is often overlooked, or people might not comprehend its importance, but it makes most of the difference when it comes to bulk buying. Buying groceries for weekly use is one thing, but to stock them for a month or more can be a big burden on your wallet, and you cannot spend all your money on food when there is a crisis. Therefore, the food we plan to stock for such a condition must also be budget-friendly and cost-effective. It does not have to be cheap and low-quality, but the packaging must be of good quality and reasonable pricing.

There are certain ways in which you can buy and store lots of non-perishable food items without feeling a financial burden or strain. First, prepare the list of all the items needed for storage and write down the total amount required. Then divide the total amount into weeks, set a target to buy 25 or 50 percent extra groceries every week, and then stock that extra in your pantry. In this way, your overall financial burden will be divided, and it will take minimum time and effort to stock food on a weekly basis.

This practice can also be carried out on normal days to keep your food secure all the time.

Meals Ready to Eat

While not all survival food items are termed as MREs (meals ready to eat), it is also not a standard food selection standard, but it is important to discuss this concept here, as many preppers commonly use MREs for survival storage. It is mostly utilized by the people who are constantly traveling in a crisis or going to places where there is no food supply. MREs are ready-to-eat meals available in sealed packages. Inside of one is a variety of food items that can provide much-needed calories, carbohydrates, fats, fibers, proteins, etc.

While the idea of having a well processed, healthy, and variety of food in a single package seems tempting, MREs are only suitable for those who cannot manage to stock or who don't have the resources to stock food. These packages are comparatively expensive and will cost you more than the raw non-perishable food. The only advantage these ready-to-eat meals have is that they can be consumed instantly without cooking, and they are rich in nutrients. These packages work well for emergency stockpiling, and for survival food storage, you can buy a few MREs (if affordable) just in case times get really difficult.

Healthy

Just because there is a crisis and you need to survive for a longer period of time with survival food, it does not mean that you can compromise the quality of the food you're eating. In fact, biological science tells you that the human body needs more calories and nutrients to sustain and live a healthy life in a crisis condition. For this reason, the food that we are storing for such conditions much be rich in nutrients. It must be better in quality than the food we normally eat. There are several perishable food items that we wouldn't be able to consume during the crisis, so the food that we are going to consume must be capable of providing the nutrients of those perishable items as well.

For instance, we cannot consume fresh meat and milk while living on survival food. The protein intake must be met by consuming high protein non-perishable items like grains, legumes, protein powders, dry egg supplements, etc. Similarly, other minerals, vitamins, and fibers widely present in fresh vegetables and fruits must be consumed through canned vegetables, fruits, psyllium husk, whole wheat flour, dried herbs, and dehydrated food products. The food that is stored must contain a perfect balance of all the macro and micronutrients.

Variety

It is natural to get bored and lose your morale during crisis conditions. And if your food is also not attractive, fun, and exciting, you will soon lose your appetite. Indeed, living on survival food is not easy, and it comes with all forms of challenges, but you can turn it around and make things exciting by keeping variety in the stocked food. In fact, most of the food that we can store for this purpose comes in wide varieties, which can store to make a range of different meals. Take legumes, for instance, and you can stock yellow, brown, red, orange, green, and white lentils, then use each to cook various meals. You can use the same lentils for cooking soups, stews, gravies, and snacks.

Having variety in survival food is not an option—it is an absolute need! You can maintain this variety by keeping different seasonings, spices, condiments, a variety of grains, pasta, and beans, etc. By employing different cooking methods, the same food can be cooked repeatedly in different ways. Use slow cooking, stewing, fermentation, baking, or other cooking styles for cooking the basic combination of ingredients. Mix and match one type of seasoning with a different type of grain. Make use of rice and bread to prepare different servings every time. You'll need to be as creative as possible in order to keep the menu fun and exciting.

Chapter 3

Food Storage Equipment, Tips, and Kits

Proper storage is all that is important when it comes to survival food. The importance of storage is greater when we are opting for a long duration storage program. We need appropriate containers, which could prevent food from all the factors stated above. There are several options on the list to use for storage purposes. In order to select the best possible container, you must consider the quantity of the food and its composition.

Cans

When it comes to storing dry, low oil, shelf-stable food, cans can be used effectively for long-term dry storage. Cans only retain 10 percent or less moisture inside. The material of a can is also unreactive, so the food does not react with the metal.

Cans come in a variety of shapes and sizes. Enamel coating inside the cans is not hazardous for the food either. The largest-sized cans can store as much as three quarts of food inside. You can store one pound of dried sliced apple, two pounds of dry onions, five and a half pounds of wheat, and four pounds of white flour in these cans. The only downside of the cans is that they can gradually erode due to rust if kept in a humid environment. Therefore, it is advised to keep the cans away from any possible source of moisture.

Foil Pouches/Mylar Bags

Then comes the foil bags or pouches, which are made out of several layers of aluminum and food-grade plastic. They practically keep the food safe from extra heat, contamination, and moisture. Food cannot react with the aluminum because it is linked with the food-grade plastic on the inside. It is important to buy quality pouches to ensure safe and healthy food storage. Low-quality pouches come with poor quality plastic lining, contaminating the food with chemicals, microplastic, and carcinogens.

High-quality mylar or aluminum bags are, therefore, recommended. The bags are available in various sizes, from a seven-milliliter Ziploc bag to a quart, gallon, pint, and five-gallon sizes, you can use any depending on the amount of the food.

Once these bags are sealed, they do not allow insects or moisture to get through its aluminum sheets. You can also use these bags for the double lining of the food; keep the

food in the aluminum bags first, then seal it inside the sealable buckets or containers.

This method is especially useful when you want to keep your food away from rodents. The aluminum bags have only one disadvantage: they cannot protect against rodents, so the double storage method can help resolve this problem quite conveniently.

Polyethylene Terephthalate-Plastic Bottles

Clean and dry PETE bottles are appropriate to store dry food products like lentils, legumes, dry beans, grains like rice, wheat, barley, oats, etc. Any other type of plastic is not good enough to prevent moisture and oxygen from getting into the food. You can identify PETE plastic bottles by reading the PETE or PET sign written under the bottles' recyclable symbol. Similarly, soda pop bottles are another good option for long-term storage. The plastic of these bottles minimizes contamination and also keeps the food chemical-free. The best part is that the bottles are reusable, and you can use them multiple times for storing non-perishable dry food items.

Plastic Buckets

If you are stocking food for three, six, or twelve months, you will need larger containers, such as these plastic buckets. These containers are specially made out of food-grade plastic, and the lid on top of the bucket is installed with a gasket seal, which keeps the food safe and secure inside.

These plastic buckets are useful for bulk grain storage. But any basket made out of nonfood-grade material, or if it has been used to store nonfood items before, is not suitable for food storage. Hence, they must be avoided.

Another advantage of using sealable food buckets is that you can use them to hoard multiple dry items in a single place by individually packing them in mylar bags or food-grade plastic bags; these items may include sugar, pasta, salt, baking powder, other dry spices, etc. All the food buckets are lined from the inside out, keeping the moisture away and not allowing it to get to the food. However, there is a possible risk of insect growth inside if you leave the bucket in a warm and humid place for longer durations.

Glass Jars

Glass jars are the most suitable reusable storage container, appropriate for long- and short-term storage. Firstly, glass does not react with the food, so there are zero percent chances of contamination. Moisture cannot get through the thick layer of the glass, and the lid of these containers is designed with a sealable gasket to allow complete sealing of the food inside. Jars are not only good to store dry food items like grains, dry spices, lentils, legumes, etc., but they are also great for storing sauces and condiments.

Chapter 4

Food for 72-Hour Emergency Kits

A state of emergency is a situation that happens by uncommon occurrences and unusual natural events with limited facilities that bind the circle of living. And the most valuable material in such a situation is essential for humans; no doubt, it is food. And when we need to manage a 72-hour emergency kit, we are bound to choose healthy food that is perpetual, easy to pack, and demands little time to cook, if any. As it is known, consuming plenty of salty foods and caffeinated beverages can increase fluid in the body, which contributes to dehydration, so it is imperative to conserve water during periods of shortage.

The best foods for your emergency kit are listed below.

1. Baby food or formula

2. Beef jerky

3. Canned fruits and vegetables

4. Canned meats (like tuna, chicken)

5. Canned or bottled juices

6. Comfort foods (like cookies or chocolate)

7. Dried fruit

8. Granola bars or protein bars

9. Instant coffee or tea

10. Nuts

11. Powdered soup mixes

12. Powdered drink mixes (like Gatorade)

13. Peanut butter and crackers

14. Shelf-stable milk

15. Whole-grain cereal

It is necessary to note that your power and water will likely be out, so buy a manual can opener and disposable eating utensils. For cooking and heating water, you probably need a mini stove while camping.

Chapter 5

Food for Short-Term Emergencies: Two Weeks to Three Months

Taking an emergency food kit for two weeks to three months directly depends on storage capacity. And organizing it nicely is a challenging task to do. Its prime need is to manage all the cans and food with the space you have. Applying the "first in, first out" method can become disorganized when dealing with canned food. Various canned food organizers and rotators for assistance can be found easily on web stores these days. Those help you manage your canned food and work well to rotate cans for "first-in, first-out."

The Desorbs Stackable Can Rack is suitable, and you can easily find it on web stores like Amazon. It provides adjustable plastic dividers, making it able to accommodate different can sizes. This canned food organizer will help you build your three-month food supply and make organizing asë easy as it is at your fingertips.

The best foods for your three-month emergency kit are listed below.

1. Apple sauce

2. Canned meat (tuna, chicken, beef stew, Spam, etc.)

3. Canned vegetables (green beans, peas, corn, tomatoes, etc.)

4. Canned fruit (peaches, pineapple, pears, etc.)

5. Canned fruit and vegetables

6. Flour, yeast, and baking powder

7. Packages of bottled water, gallon jugs of water

8. Packets of oatmeal or just oats

9. Pancake mix

10. Pasta and spaghetti sauce

11. Peanut butter

12. Pinto or other types of beans

13. Powdered drink mix

14. Salt and favorite seasonings

15. Snacks, granola bars

16. Soup or broth

17. White or wheat rice

Chapter 6

Food for Long-Term Emergencies: Three Months to a Year

Before preparing for survival food stocking, every prepper must have a complete and full-fledged list of all the food items that must be bought. The food must be categorized and grouped in a well-written list so that the prepper remains oriented during grocery shopping. In this chapter, all the survival food items are discussed in much detail. Each sub-section comprises one category of a storage food item, its storable varieties, and ways to store for long-term durations. At the end of this chapter, you will get a survival food checklist, which will let you know about the quantities of the food you will need for a certain duration of storage.

Canned Liquids

Canned food products have a longer shelf life as they are prepared using various preservatives. If you want to stock otherwise perishable food items like pineapples, olives, or vegetables, then store them in their canned forms. These canned products must have a higher liquid proportion so that the food would provide you a good amount of nutrients and ensure hydration as well. You can also store various liquids in the sealed cans like coconut milk, condensed milk, and evaporated milk. Other food items that can make a good canned product for your survival stock include vegetables, chicken and beef stock, broths, stewed or crushed tomatoes, etc.

Distilled And Seltzer Water

Though water is not food, it is still the basic necessity of every individual. We can probably survive days without food, but we certainly cannot survive without water. Moreover, water is also largely used in cooking. If you fear the crisis could make you water-deprived, then you must have a sufficient amount of water stored in your pantry. Distilled or seltzer water is appropriate for long-term storage. Make sure to store water in a sealed bucket or PETE bottles, away from all other stored food items.

Powdered Milk, Whey, and Eggs

As we know, fresh animal milk cannot be stored for more than three days in the refrigerator or more than a week or two in the freezer, and for long-term storage, we can't have fresh milk on the list. It must be replaced with other non-perishable options with a greater shelf life that includes all forms of dehydrated, powdered milk. It is a good substitute for fresh milk. But make sure to get yourself quality milk powder and avoid buying tea whiteners, which are neither healthy nor nutritious.

Like powdered milk, there are other powdered substitutes available that easily replace certain dairy products. Vegan egg powder substitutes are available, which provides the same amount of nutrients as an egg. Whey protein powder can also be stored as a survival food to maintain optimum protein intake.

Hard Cheeses

Not all varieties of cheese are suitable for long-term storage. The only variety you can store at home is the waxed hard cheese, though you will have a hard time finding this cheese; all your efforts are worth this highly nutritious and rich waxed cheese. This cheese is enclosed in a wax sheath, which prevents bacteria and mold growth while keeping the moisture away from the cheese inside. The hard Parmesan cheese in powdered form has only four months of shelf life, but it can last fresh for twenty-five years if packed in a wax case. Wax-encased Gouda, sharp cheddar, swiss, and Kraft Parmesan cheese are options you should look for.

Protein Bars and Drinks

Since it is not ideal to store fresh meat products as survival food, protein intake can be compromised on this survival food menu. For this reason, protein intake must be maintained by consuming protein via protein bars or drinks. These items are available in dry forms, which can be easily stored in a refrigerator or some other dry and cool place inside your pantry. You should be looking for high-energy protein-rich bars that have a longer shelf life.

Canned Dehydrated Meats

Storing meat in its fresh form is not on the card. Unless you have a freezer spared for meat storage, you cannot even think of storing meat for long periods of time. Even in the freezer, meat can only last fresh for about three or four weeks. However, we can easily store another substitute that can provide good taste and protein content. Such meat items include all the canned and dehydrated varieties. For instance, canned tuna can be stored in the refrigerator, or you can make jerky to enjoy the meat every now and then on the survival food diet.

Drink Mixes

You can't have fresh drinks and juices on the survival food stockpile. The closest substitute to those drinks is ready-to-make powdered drink mixes. These powdered mixes come in various flavors, including pineapple, apple, mango, orange, lemon, etc. You can simply mix and drink them for a refreshing experience. Similarly, other dry drink substitutes can be added to the survival food stock.

They mainly include tea leaves, coffee beans, and powder. There is an endless variety of tea that you can add to the menu, such as black tea, chamomile, cardamom tea, green tea, earl grey, lemongrass, etc.

Tea, especially green tea, is full of antioxidants, and it has natural healing properties. Lastly, coffee is a good addition to the stock as it has a longer shelf life, and when kept in a dry and cool place, the beans remain fresh. Brewed coffee is an energy booster and can be used in other drinks and desserts as well.

Oils

Cooking is not possible with some use of fats or cooking oils, and your survival food stock is also incomplete without sufficient oil storage. Since cooking oils and other fats can sustain well at room temperature, you can easily store them in large plastic buckets or PETE bottles. Vegetable or plant-based cooking oils are healthier options to look for. Olive oil, organic fat shortening, or lard are a few other options for long-term storage. If cooking oil is stored properly in a clean and sealable container, it won't go bad for as long as two years. Solid fats like butter, lard, and shortening should be kept in the refrigerator if the atmospheric temperature is high.

Whole Wheat Flour

Another survival food item that you can store in your pantry with complete ease is dry flour. Whole wheat flour is considered the most appropriate as it is rich in fiber and other nutrients. It can be stored fresh from four to six months in a moisture-free, cool, and dark place. However, if you are buying other packaged flour, go by the package's expiration date. Similarly, you can also store rice or chickpea flour, but to prevent these powdered grains from developing insects over time, try the dry ice method to remove all the moisture or add desiccants to the storage containers. Besides flour, you can also store packaged cake mix, pancake mix, or bread mix. Leave them sealed in their market-bought pouches until you are ready to use them. Buy small single-use packets or pouches.

Cereal

Whole grains, shredded wheat, and cereal are some of the best survival food as they are loaded with energy and nutrients and are low-maintenance stock food. You can find nearly all the nutrients you need in cereal and grains: proteins, fibers, carbohydrates, folate, selenium, vitamin

E, manganese, magnesium, and zinc. So, it is recommended to store them in a large amount in dry and clean sealable containers.

The best practice is to store them in small sealable food-grade plastic bags according to each week's need, then stock these bags in an orderly manner.

In this way, the rest of the packed cereal and grains will remain safe as they will not be exposed to the moisture repeatedly.

Potato Flour

Storing potato flour in your pantry will help you in the long run. You can keep it as a backup if you run out of wheat-based flour; you can then use it to prepare dough and batter. Since it can absorb moisture well, it makes a nice yeast dough.

Corn as a Grain

You cannot store fresh corn or corn cobs for more than a few days. Canned corn is fresh for a few weeks. But the same corn, when dried, can be stored for months. Dried corn comes in a variety of forms like corn flour, cornflakes, and cornmeal. All the dry varieties can be easily stored in their company packaging or a sealable jar. Corn flour is used in baking, or as a thickening agent, whereas cornmeal can be used to make bread and cake.

Oats and Oatmeal

How can we forget long-lasting oats and oatmeal? This survival food is a must to become a part of your pantry storage as it can easily make you get through difficult times due to its high nutritional value. Oats make a good and nourishing breakfast. If you can't find anything quick and easy to serve at the tables, then cook delicious oatmeal in just twelve minutes. The oatmeal recipes do not even call for a large number of ingredients as they can be easily cooked in water or milk.

Bread Crumbs

Another good survival food option that you can store in your pantry with complete ease without the fear of early spoilage is bread crumbs. That's right! Bread crumbs are already dry, and they are packed in sealed pouches. You can either directly stock the pouches or keep the crumbs sealed in a glass jar. Let's face it, bread crumbs are a part of every other crusted meal, so we can't get really crispy food without some use of them. It is wise to store them for longer-term use. Make sure to keep the crumbs away from moisture, or else they will lose their crisp.

Meals Ready to Eat

Also known as MREs, these are often recommended on the survival food diet. The concept emerged from the military ready-to-eat meals, which are often sent along with military personnel to places where there is no food availability. These packaged items have a longer shelf life. Now MREs are also manufactured for civilians, but a complete package can cost more than other survival food on this list. The meal comes in a complete package with a variety of shelf-stable food inside like jams, canned meat, sauces, pureed fruits, vegetables, etc.

Crackers and Cookies

Though crackers and cookies are not healthy, they can keep your survival food diet fun and exciting. Crises can be nerve-racking, and crackers or cookies are a perfect way to feel good about it—store small packets of crackers and cookies in a variety of flavors. While buying the cookies, make sure to get those that have a relatively greater nutritional value and a longer shelf life. Cream and butter cookies do not stay good at room temperature, so if you are planning to store them, then either freeze or refrigerate them in a clean, sealable container.

Rice

Both beans and rice are the staples of every stockpile diet. When you are buying rice for survival food storage, jasmine rice is a good option as it is good in quality and comparatively cheap. Additionally, you can try other varieties of white rice, like short-grain Asian rice, wild rice, or Italian Arborio rice. Using the diverse varieties of rice, you can make different meals. White rice is preferred over brown rice as white rice does not take much of the cooking resources to cook as brown rice. Rice flour and popper rice can also be kept in the pantry, provided you keep them dry and clean.

Ideal for long-term storage, dry pasta can be stored for a month without spoilage, and it is a good source of instant energy. It requires minimum resources, and you can boil it in just a few minutes. Pasta is available in a wide variety, so we recommend dividing your overall pasta needs according to these varieties. You can store dried tortellini, couscous, orzo, egg noodles, fettuccine, gnocchi, spaghetti, lasagna strips, macaroni, penne, mostaccioli, linguine, rigatoni, and rotini. Then there are soba buckwheat noodles, rice noodles, chow mein, and bean curd noodles; perhaps you can store all of its endless varieties for months and even an entire year. The downside is that pasta is also prone to insect attacks like other grains, so it should be stored in an absolutely moisture-free space.

Raisins, Dried Fruits, and Fruit Strips

Processed dried fruits are a rich source of energy and other nutrients. Dried fruits like raisins, apricots, cranberries, dates, and mangos can be easily stored in sealable Ziploc bags or market-bought packages. Aluminum pouches with food-grade plastic lining are most suitable to store the dried fruits, whether separately or in trail mix form. Raisins and currants should be stored in a large amount for survival storage as they are full of iron, proteins, fiber, vitamin C, potassium, and antioxidants. From cookies to bread, muffins, desserts, and breakfast oatmeal, raisins can be added to enhance the flavor and nutritional content.

Jams and Jellies

There is yet another way to extend the shelf life of fruit and convert their flesh and pulp to jellies and jams. Once cooked into jams, the fruit can last for months. For this reason, jam and jellies are also added to the ready-to-eat meals (MREs). You can store raspberry, blackberry, and strawberry jams.

Apple butter, apple sauce, or grape jellies are good to store for long-term survival storage. PETE bottles and sealable mason jars are most appropriate to preserve these jams and jellies. Keep the storage containers away from heat and light.

Canned Fruits

Fruits contain more calories than vegetables, and therefore it is important to keep as many fruit-based items stored in the survival stockpile. Instead of fresh fruits, go for the canned fruits, which are packed in syrups and liquids inside a can. Fruit packed with liquid provides calories, nutrients, and hydrates as well. Pineapple, mandarins, cherries, pumpkin puree, etc., all come in a sealed can, and you can keep them stored for up to three months in the refrigerator.

Canned Veggies

Since fresh vegetables are also crossed off the survival food list, we are left with canned options. Fortunately, there are several canned vegetables available in the market. Canned green beans, olives, artichokes, asparagus, beets, cabbage, and sauerkraut are all easily available in stores.

Beans and Legumes

One cannot overemphasize the importance of legumes and beans. Whether dried or canned, beans prove to be a high-energy survival food. This category includes a number of varieties: chickpeas, black-eyed peas, split peas, kidney beans, white beans, cannellini beans, etc. A pack of beans can provide as many as 1,250 calories per pound. Moreover, you can pair them with ingredients in several ways to enjoy a new meal every time. Beans and legumes grow in plants' roots; that is why they are stored with carbohydrates, protein, essential oils, fiber, vitamins, minerals, and phytonutrients. In their dried form, beans can be stocked for three to six months.

Nuts, Seeds, and Nut Butter

All nuts and seeds are known as little power boosters. Though used in small amounts, nuts and seeds can provide the most energy and calories. They are dense and rich in nutrients, so they be must be stocked in the pantry in a good amount. Commonly used seeds include sunflower seeds, pumpkin seeds, hemp, flaxseeds, etc. Nuts and seeds can go rancid in a month or two, so they must be used in rotation. Add cashews, walnuts, and almonds to the stockpile. Roast varieties or nuts are considered more appropriate for long-term storage, including Brazil nuts, pine nuts, hazelnuts, pecans, etc. If you fear that these nuts will go rancid after a month, store other nut-based alternatives with a relatively long shelf life like peanut butter, almond butter, nut bars, etc.

Honey

If you like the idea of storing something healthy in your survival food stockpile, then store a good amount of honey. We know that honey is produced in a natural environment, and it does not go bad at room temperature, even for months. So, instead of using other artificial and unhealthy sweeteners, keep honey in your pantry. It is not only good and mildly sweet, but adds a nice flavor to all your desserts, smoothies, drinks, and bread. It is important to check the quality of honey; it has to be 100 percent pure in order to sustain long-term storage. Keep it sealed in a tightly closed jar or bottle in a dry and cool place.

Iodized Salt

Salt is the natural balancer of sodium in the body. Without cooking, it is almost impossible from seasoning to curing, pickling, and marination, salt is used in all the processes, and thus there must be a sufficient stockpile of salt in the pantry. Iodized salt is recommended for daily usage, as well as for storage. Such salt prevents thyroid-related disorders like goiter. Besides iodized salt, there are other varieties of salt that every prepper should stock for long-term usage. Canning and pickling salt is a granulated form of pure salt with additives and preservatives.

Then comes the pink Himalayan salt, which is rich in minerals, copper, iron, potassium, calcium, and magnesium, and it has a peculiar taste, entirely different from table salt. Epsom salt is yet another variety that is good for digestion and for the skin as well.

Sugars and Molasses

Sugars and molasses are another important part of the routine diet, and one cannot simply stock food without storing a good amount of sugar. Thankfully, sugar does not demand much maintenance, and if you are keeping it moisture-free, and away from insects and mites, it will last for as long as you want. It can be bought in bags and pouches, but the best way to store sugar in bulk is by using mylar containers or plastic buckets. Take large-sized containers with sealable gasket lids having five gallons or more of the volume, and then add sugar to this container. Keep it tightly sealed.

Spices and Herbs

Even during a crisis, you cannot think of having tasteless food. We all want some flavors and aroma in every meal. Therefore, spices and herbs should be stored as well to make those rice and beans tasty. All dried herbs, ranging from dried rosemary to oregano, dill, and thyme, are shelf-stable. They can be easily stored in a sealable bottle, even in your kitchen cabinets. Spices like crushed or powdered red pepper, cumin, dried mustard, garlic powder, onion powder, ginger powder, chili, and saffron are also good to store for long durations. As long as you keep the spices and herbs moisture-free, you can enjoy them for months.

Condiments

Remember that not all condiments are not shelf-stable, and some even go bad when left at room temperature. But condiments are an essential part of our meals, so we can store some in canned varieties. Pickle relish, Dijon mustard, and canned mayonnaise make for good survival food. It's the same with sugar-free ketchup and other sauces. These condiments are only suitable for short-term storage, probably for one to three months, provided that they are kept in a cool place like a refrigerator. Soy sauce, Tabasco sauce, and Worcestershire sauce can also be stored in clean PETE bottles to flavor soups, stews, and gravies.

Chocolate

Surprise! Surprise! Now you can enjoy chocolate even on your survival food stock. Since chocolate-based products are sustainable, they can be stored for about a year in cool and dry places. Whether it's dry cocoa powder, chocolate chips, or chocolate syrup, they all are good power boosters containing lots of antioxidants, which is exactly what we need on this diet. The chocolate you are buying to store should be pure, and it must have minimum sugar or milk content. Dark and semi-sweet chocolate is more preferable for storage purposes.

Apple Cider Vinegar and Other Vinegar

Among the few last things that you can store in your pantry is apple cider vinegar. This vinegar is a result of the fermentation process, so it can practically last fresh in your pantry without much effort. Apple cider vinegar has numerous health advantages, and you can add it to a number of drinks, soups, stews, marinades, and salads. Buy a couple of apple cider vinegar bottles and keep them in your pantry. Balsamic and rice wine vinegar are other good options for storage.

Vanilla Extract

Since the vanilla extract is commonly used in baking and cooking and has a longer shelf life, you can store three of four bottles in your pantry for occasional use. It's not just vanilla extract that you can store, as there are several other extracts that you can now store from one to three months, like cocoa extras, peppermint essence, banana extract, etc. Keep these bottles in a cabinet or a shelf where it is dark and comparatively cool.

Leavening Agents

Leavening agents are used in preparing the dough for various kinds of bread. These agents help raise the dough and make it soft and fluffy after baking. Since leavening agents are important in cooking, they must also be stocked in the pantry. Commonly used leavening agents are dry yeast, baking powder, and baking soda. Baking soda and baking powder are both dry white powders, which can be easily stored in small spice bottles or PETE bottles. If you are keeping them moisture-free, they do not expire for more than a year.

Yeast comes in three different varieties: fresh yeast, instant yeast, and active dry yeast. When it comes to stockpiling, I often recommend everyone to store active dry yeast, and it is available in a granule; it is quite effective and needs rehydration for activation, whereas instant yeast can also be used as a substitute and can be stored in small aluminum packets or spice bottles.

Chapter 7

Ways to Cook Emergency Kit Food

As long as you can make a fire, you can cook food anywhere. If you are prepared for emergencies or any crisis, you will have all the different tools and equipment to cook food. Using your emergency kit, you can prepare all sorts of meals. There are different methods that you can resort to during emergencies, and those include the following.

Mixing and Blending

Food items stored in powdered forms like powdered juice mix, powdered milk, protein, and shake mixes can be prepared by mixing them with liquid like water or canned milk. Extra ingredients like seasonings, flavorings, nuts, dry or canned fruits, etc., can also be added to the blends. It is advised to keep a mini portable blender or a shaker in the emergency kits so you can easily mix and blend all the ingredients together during emergencies and serve instantly.

Ash Cakes

The campfire can be utilized to cook various meals, and the rocks that are heated with this fire can be used to bake bread. Having no oven will not be a problem, because you can bake the bread by setting the dough on the hot rocks placed near the campfire.

Cooking with Foil

A foil sheet really comes in handy when it comes to cooking in an emergency. It is easy to store, does not take a lot of storage space, and you can use or shape the sheet in different containers, cooking pans, etc.

Portable Folding Stoves

If you can, buy any of those portable stoves that come with campfire fuel. These stoves can be set anywhere, and you can easily ignite them by using their fuel refills. They are great for cooking food in small pans and griddles. The good thing about these stoves is that they are space friendly and affordable as well.

Roasting on Firepits

Roasting on the fire is how our ancestors used to do it. So, we can try the same and cook all sorts of meat and veggies by threading them on the skewers and then roast them on the fire. Mini, portable, and easy to carry and store metal or iron pits are widely available these days, so you can buy them and store them along with some wood or coal to create fire whenever needed.

Solar Oven

It is a solar-powered oven, which is not available for everyone, but if you are planning for emergencies, then having this oven with you will greatly help as it will save you from covering yourself in smoke.

Reflecting Oven

These are some simple ovens that can be created on the ground to focus the heat to a central area to bake food. It is usually designed in such shape and size that it makes cooking easier.

Griddles

Skillets, griddles, and frying pans will let you make tasty meals resembling home-cooked food. You can use stones, bricks, cinderblocks, or other supports to provide a good base for the griddle or frying pan over a small fire.

Kelly Kettle

These kettles make coffee-making quite convenient. Moreover, they are great for heating water for all purposes. These kettles can hold up to seven cups of water and heat them in just a few minutes.

Solo Stove

These are metallic stoves with spaces to add twigs, pinecones, wood, or leaves to burn as fuel. They are more effective than the canister fuel-based stoves.

Volcano Collapsible Cook Stove

These stoves provide effective heating and can be used to burn all of the easily available fuels like wood, charcoal, and propane.

Can Camp Stove

Used tin cans are excellent to turn into camp stoves. All you need is some wood chips or any other dry fuel to light it up. Try using multiple cans to make a stable base for cooking.

Chapter 8

Preserving Your Own Food

Even with a long shelf life, survival food cannot last fresh for long unless stored properly. Food storage is central to this process. Otherwise, the whole effort of stocking up the food will prove pointless. There are several variables and factors that come into play; food storage is not as simple as stocking up items in a sealed container or bags. Food storage has a science of its own, and it requires a complete understanding of the items that are used and stockpiled. In this chapter, we shall look into all the variables responsible for food spoilage and how they can be prevented using effective techniques.

Determining the period of food storage is the basic step of this whole process. When you decide on the duration of storage, set the right trajectory, making storage convenient, effective, and easy. It is said that stocking food in great bulk without analyzing the situation will end in complete failure and massive food spoilage. The smart move is always to start from small achievable targets and then move towards something big; in other words, start with short-term food storage and then gradually shift towards long-term storage. And if you haven't stockpiled food before, this basic technique will save you from unwanted errors and mistakes. You can store food in a progressive manner in the following stages.

1 Month

The best practice is to store the food for one month first. It is comparatively easier to manage to stockpile for one month only, and it also costs less. This method works well for a short-term crisis. To stock food for a month, you can either buy groceries for a month in the one visit, or you can continue buying 25 percent extra groceries along with your weekly grocery shopping and continue saving and storing this extra proportion according to appropriate preservation and storage techniques. Every time you buy additional food for storage, store it right away in clean and sealable containers with appropriate labels in a suitable space; this will save you from spending countless hours in your kitchen and the pantry. The whole struggle of food storage will then be divided into one day a week, and at the end of the month, you will have to store food for the entire next month. This one-month storage program can be repeated when it is possible to buy new groceries. The added advantage of this process is that you will have more space to store food. Space can be easily managed inside kitchen cabinets, for example. In this method, items with relatively shorter shelf life can also be stocked.

3 Months

If one-month buying does not bring you convenience, and bulk buying is the absolute need of the hour, then three months of storage is another smart strategy to store food. But remember that you will have a lot of food to store in this case, which will require an equally larger space in your house.

So, if you are planning to stockpile for three months, then first prepare and plan how to create an appropriate space for the food. Any space designated as survival food must be divided into subspaces in which a specific category of food could be stored according to the required conditions.

For instance, if you don't have a large freezer at home, you will not be able to store too many frozen products. Your pantry must have a dry environment and low temperatures to keep grains and legumes safe. Items with a relatively longer shelf life have to be stored for a three-month duration. Moreover, the stocked food items also need to be frequently checked and monitored every two weeks or month to track their condition and utility.

6 Months

Six months of storage works for a long-term crisis and ensures food security for half of the year. The idea is to store such items of basic need, which could guarantee better health and survival. It would require a bigger space to arrange and store the stock for six months. You can start stocking one category of food at a time, then move to the next. Large containers and boxes should be bought to conveniently store all the food. Solid, dry, and raw cooking items are most suitable for six months of storage, including wheat grains, rice, salt, sugar, lentils, etc. Frozen items cannot last fresh for more than six months in the freezer, so it requires extra care while storing such items. It is advisable to store only frozen items for the first three months of this duration.

1 year

The one-year storage may seem a difficult task, but it is the only method that ensures food security the most. Every nitty-gritty part of the process must be carefully planned before opting for this method of storage. Smart grocery shopping and gradual storage will make this kind of storage possible. You cannot simply buy and store groceries for an entire year overnight; it will definitely take days, weeks, and months of preparations and gradual smart buying over this period. The one-year storage method is the last stage, which must be opted for by people who are good at food management and understand the technicalities of long-duration food storage. That is why it is suggested to start from short- to long-term storage.

The storage duration is just one of the factors that must be considered during the whole stockpiling process. The above-described methods are tried and tested techniques of storage that many people have tried. It all depends on us, how we put these methods to use, and decide which method is most suitable for our crisis conditions. When it comes to food storage, mere stockpiling is not enough; the person stocking the food must also ensure the food is secure and safe in the storage, or else all of those efforts will end in vain.

Methods of Food Preservation

Learning preservation techniques is the most important part of food management, especially when you are planning to stock for weeks, months, or even a year. The food preservation methods that we can use at home are all conventional and tested by many. The bottom line is to prevent the growth of microbes or other living organisms inside the food we are about to store. Items that are commonly stored as survival food include raw lentils, legumes, spices, and grains, along with frozen meat and dairy products. Such items' shelf life varies considerably, but we can ensure longer shelf life by using different traditional and old-school methods of preservation.

Vacuum Sealing

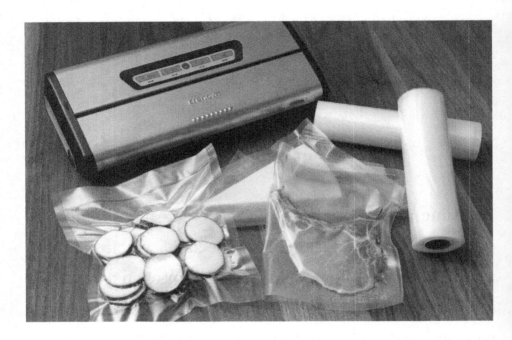

Air is the major carrier of oxygen, moisture, and contaminants that spoils the food. The basic concept of this method is that if we successfully prevent the air from reaching the food, we can reduce early spoilage risks. For this reason, vacuum sealing is used for all types of food items, whether perishable or non-perishable; in both cases, the shelf life of the food is extended. This method can be applied to the food items that are stored in mylar or aluminum bags. The vacuum is artificially created inside the bag by removing all the air inside. To do so, first, take a clean and food-grade aluminum pouch or mylar bag, then place the food inside the bag. Now hold the sealable edges of the bag in your hands and submerge the rest of the bag in a bucket full of water; the air leaves the bag as it is lighter, and the water outside the bag exerts pressure. Once the air is removed, seal the bag immediately and store it in the refrigerator, freezer, or any other suitable place.

Dry Ice Process

The dry ice technique also works on a similar concept, and in this method, the effort is made to remove oxygen from the food. Whether you are storing food in a bag, PETE bottle, or food bucket, you can easily use this method and ensure the minimum growth of microbes and insects inside the food. Dry ice is basically carbon dioxide, which is heavier than oxygen. So, remove the oxygen from the food. The storage bucket is placed in another larger bucket filled with dry ice, and the oxygen leaves the bucket due to its lighter weight. Then you can seal the lid to store the food for long durations.

Oxygen Absorbers

There is yet another technique that can remove oxygen from food and prevent insects' growth inside the containers, and it is the use of oxygen absorbers. They are considered even more effective than the vacuum sealing method. Oxygen absorbers are small packets that contain iron powder, and the packets are made out of such materials that they absorb oxygen and moisture but do not allow the iron or other chemicals to leak out of the bags. Therefore, they are considered safe for human health. These bags are most appropriate for places where there is more humidity and a greater chance of oxidation.

Freezing Method

Freezing can keep even the perishable food items like meat, dairy, vegetables, and fruits stored fresh for as long as three months. And it is one of the most effective methods to extend the shelf life of all the survival food items. It is mainly because freezing drops the food's temperature below zero degrees, which ceases the microbial growth and prevents spoilage.

The texture, taste, and nutrients of the food are also preserved.

Use Desiccants

Like silica gel, desiccants work similarly to the oxygen absorbers, except they absorb the moisture instead of absorbing oxygen. Places with a naturally humid environment cannot ensure moisture-free air to the food stored even when properly sealed in the containers, so it is always at the risk of oxidation or fungal growth. By placing silica gel packed in small bags, the moisture is effectively absorbed into this desiccant while leaving the food moisture-free.

Pickling

Pickling is one of the most traditional methods of preserving a variety of food, especially fruits and vegetables. As they rot quickly, it was a major issue of ancient times to keep them stored for a longer duration. And pickling was discovered as an appropriate method that prevented the fruits and vegetables from spoilage and ensured good taste and nutrients.

The process works because it does not allow microbes to grow within the food. The items are submerged in the liquid, which has a high concentration of salts, spices, sugar, or citric acid. The environment thus created around the food is best to prevent microbial growth. Once pickled, the food takes on a rich and concentrated flavor but tends to remain edible, which is the end goal here. That is why pickling can be employed to store food if desired.

Dehydrating

The process is used to remove all the moisture from the food. Dehydration is not new, and it has been in use for centuries. It enables you to preserve a variety of food items from dehydrated vegetables, meats, spices, and fruits. Dehydration simply extends the shelf life of the food and prevents microbial growth. The question is, how exactly can we dehydrate the food, and will it remain the same after dehydration? The taste and texture of the food definitely change after the dehydration process, but its nutritional value is preserved. Food with higher water content like vegetables and fruits is usually reduced in volume and enriched in nutrients. Even a small amount of such dehydrated food items is sufficient to meet your caloric needs. The reduction in volume also allows you to store a large amount of food in a smaller space.

Dehydrating is carried out at extremely low temperatures so that the food is not cooked, but it only loses its moisture. Such a low temperature is difficult to maintain manually. Therefore, there are dehydrators available to carry out this task for you. Using these dehydrators makes it easier to control the low temperature and manage the dehydration in the required time. It can also be carried out in ovens if you keep the temperature low and food away from the direct heat.

But before getting to the actual dehydration, the first step is to prepare it for the process. The science of dehydration is simple: the greater the surface area of the food and the lesser the thickness, the more moisture will be evaporated out of it. For this reason, the food must be sliced thinly. For instance, if you are dehydrating fruits and vegetables, you need to cut them into thin slices. The same is the case with meat, and it has to be cut into thin strips or slices like the beef jerky we eat. However, when extremely thin slices are dehydrated, they get super crispy and crunchy, whereas thick slices turn a bit chewy in texture. So, prepare and cut the food items according to the texture you want.

Once the food is prepared and ready for dehydration, the next step is to decide on the method of dehydration. Direct sunlight dehydration only works for certain vegetables (like peppers) but not all food items. You can remove the moisture from grains and legumes from the sunlight. However, meat and fruits must be dehydrated using dehydrators.

Slices are then placed in a single layer over the dehydrator plate. And if you want your fruits and vegetables to retain their original color even after dehydration, then drizzle some critic acid or lemon juice over the slices. The food inside is covered and left for several hours at a temperature as low as 105–130 degrees Fahrenheit. Once the food is completely dehydrated, it can be packed in a sealable clean container or plastic bag. After dehydration, the food must be kept in a dry and cool place like other non-perishable food items.

Smoking

Smoking is just another method of dehydration. Instead of drying food in an electric dehydrator or other heating appliance, the dehydration is carried out through smoking. It is most suitable to dehydrate meat as it removes moisture from the meat grains and dries out all the microbes residing on it. Direct fire smoking was the method of the past, and today it can be carried out at home using electric smokers.

Wood chips are burned to produce smoke, which infuses a strong flavor into the meat and gradually dehydrates. Meat jerky is often prepared using the smoking method. Once smoked, the jerky can then be stored without refrigeration in a clean, dry, and cool place like other non-perishable food items. As dehydration takes many hours, 24–46 at a minimum, you must prepare yourself to invest an adequate amount of time. This preservation technique cannot work for instant storage.

Root Cellars

You will probably need to build a root cellar inside the house if you plan to store your food for more than six months. This is the only way to control all the variables for better food storage. And if you live in a place where the risk of an immediate crisis and food storage is an everyday reality, then building a root cellar will save you time, effort, and money. It is usually built underground in the basement, but you can choose any cool, dark, and moisture-free place. The place must be airy and clean. It must be designed in such a way that food could be stored in an organized manner, and you can access all the items easily, besides dry grains, legumes, salt, sugar, beans, and dry spices.

Perhaps, with better storage, we can effectively store our food for a longer duration. Food management is not one formula to fit all, and you can pick and choose any of the suggested methods of preservation and select any of the storage containers depending on your need and the requirement of food. The end goal here is to maintain the quality of the food without compromising its nutritional value.

Chapter 9
Packing Dry Foods for
Long-Term Storage

Once you have decided on the total duration of food storage, the next important step is to decide where to store survival food. We have already discussed in brief that environmental conditions profoundly impact the quality of the food. Even dry and raw food grains and spices are susceptible to slow decay. And in order to keep such items safe and secure for a longer duration, one acronym must be kept in mind. HOLT corresponds to all factors that are responsible for food spoilage, and by keeping these variables under control, anyone can effectively ensure long-term survival food storage

Humidity

Just as humidity rots metallics in your house, it can also spoil your food. It is mainly because the humid environment provides microbes and fungi an optimum environment to grow. Water is essential for all life forms, and if we provide the same to the microbes, they can easily thrive on the food. Humidity can cause food spoilage even inside perfectly sealed containers if the food inside contains any traces of water. Therefore, it is important to keep the food in a place where the air is dry and moisture-free.

Oxygen

Oxygen is responsible for oxidation, which can spoil food as well as the containers the food is stored inside. This oxygen prompts rapid spoilage and attracts rodents towards the food. If the food is stored in high-quality plastic containers, there are minimum chances of oxidation, and the food inside will remain safe.

Light

We all know that light contains some amount of energy, and energy is capable of inducing changes in food over a long period of time. It changes the flavors or the color of the food if it constantly and consistently falls on the food. The degradation is slow and occurs progressively while directly affects the nutritional content of the food. That is why it is suggested to keep the food stored in a dark place, away from direct or indirect sunlight.

Temperature

Temperature plays a major role in food spoilage as bacteria, fungus, and other microbes are likely to grow at high temperatures. That is why the food cellar or pantries are built underground, as the temperature beneath the surface is lower than the atmospheric temperature. The optimum temperature to store raw solid food for a longer duration ranges between 50 to 60 degrees Fahrenheit. The temperature to store animal-based products and cooked food should be even lower to avoid bacterial contamination.

Now that you know all the important variables affecting the quality of the food, you can easily search for the right storage place. The underground basement serves as a perfect place for such storage if it is free from humidity and clean from bugs and rodents. You can also convert an empty or spare room in the house into storage.

Chapter 10

Buying Food: Budget-Friendly Ways to Stock Food Storage

Stocking of survival food requires smart and budget-friendly buying. Since you will be buying food for months or even a year, it will cost 10 to 100 times more than your monthly budget. The best way to keep this storage budget-friendly is to organize and manage everything beforehand.

1. Write down all your food needs and divide them into two categories of necessities or extras.

2. For survival storage, you will have to focus entirely on your necessities to keep the budget in control.

3. Make adjustments for the storage items and reserve some of the budget for equipment as well.

4. You can't act penny-wise and pound-foolish, analyze everything, weigh all of the pros and cons of storing certain items, and then add them to your list.

5. Divide your overall budget into sections and spend the reserved amount on each section to keep the spending under control.

6. Pack and label the items properly, then use them in rotation to avoid food spoilage and wastage of money.

Shopping List

Here is a detailed list of the food items that every prepper must stock in their pantry to maintain food security.

- Baking mixes
- Baking powder
- Baking soda
- Barley
- Bay leaves
- Beans (dry)
- Bottled drinks and juices
- Brown sugar
- Bullion, concentrated broth
- Butter flavoring

- Candy
- Canned beans
- Canned broth
- Canned chicken breast
- Canned chili
- Canned diced tomatoes
- Canned fried onions
- Canned fruit
- Canned milk, evaporated milk
- Canned pie filling
- Canned pumpkin
- Canned salmon
- Canned soups
- Canned stew
- Canned sweet potatoes
- Canned tuna
- Canned veggies
- Cans of lemonade mix
- Cheese dips in jars
- Cheese soups
- Chinese food ingredients

- Chocolate bars
- Chocolate chips
- Chocolate syrup
- Strawberry syrup squeeze bottles
- Coffee filters
- Corn Masa de Harina (corn tortilla mix)
- Cornmeal
- Corn starch for thickening
- Cream of wheat
- Cream soups
- Crisco
- Dried eggs
- Dried fruit
- Dried onion
- Dried soups
- Dry cocoa
- Dry coffee creamer
- Dry milk powder
- Dry mustard
- Flour, self-rising flour
- Garlic powder

- Granola bars
- Hard candy
- Honey
- Hot chocolate mix
- Instant coffee
- Instant mashed potatoes
- Jarred or canned spaghetti sauce
- Jarred peppers
- Jellies and jams
- Jerky
- Ketchup
- Kool-Aid
- Lard, Manteca
- Large packages of dry pasta (thinner type saves fuel)
- Marshmallow cream
- Marshmallows
- Mayo packets
- Mexican food ingredients
- Mustard
- Nestle Table Cream
- Nuts

- Oatmeal
- Oil
- Olive oil
- Olives, green and black
- Onion powder
- Packaged bread crumbs
- Pancake mix
- Parmesan
- Peanut butter
- Black pepper
- Pet food
- Pickles, relish
- Powdered sugar
- Power bars
- Raisins
- Ramen
- Ravioli
- Real butter
- Rice
- Salsa and hot sauces
- Salt

- Spices and herbs
- Stovetop Dressing mix
- Sugar
- Summer sausage
- Sweetened condensed milk
- Syrups
- Tea
- Trail mix
- Pasteurized milk
- Vanilla
- Velveeta
- Vienna sausage
- Yeast

Chapter 11
Storing Water

It might be hard to find clean water after an uncommon tragedy, and it may contaminate your regular drinking water source depending on its consequences and intensity. Prepare for an emergency by storing a supply of water that will meet the needs of you and your family members. Managing water and the way to keep it safe rely on the type of emergency. Few ways and facilities may ease you to save your water and have clean water. Bottled water is one of the best options you can choose. Unopened company mineral water is the safest and most reliable source of water in an emergency. Notice the expiration date for store-bought water. If you do not have mineral water, you can make your water safe to drink by following the listed instructions.

Following calculations are based on experiences and observations set by physicians and biologists as a recommendation. Store at least one gallon of water per day per person for drinking and sanitation. It's preferable to store a two-week supply, if possible.

If there is anyone with you who is expected to get sick, or a pregnant woman, you should consider storing more water than the above-recommended calculation. Also, consider the climate situation. If it's hot, it will cause trouble for your stored water and increase drinking demand.

There is a need to replace non-store-bought water every six months. Do not keep open water for a long time. Store a bottle of unexpired odorous, less liquid household chlorine bleach, which should say it contains 5 percent of sodium hypochlorite, to disinfect your water, if necessary. It can be used for general cleaning and sanitizing. Have a look at its expiration date and replace it on time if it's expired. Store water is the required step, which demands you to choose a container according to your requirements and needs.

When using containers to safely treat your store water for use and keep it drinkable, it is best to use food-grade storage containers that do not allow the transference of toxic substances into the water. FDA (Food and Drug Administration) approved food-grade storage containers can be easily found at camping supply stores or web stores. Make sure the one you buy is a food-grade container. If you are not able to find a food-grade water storage container, make sure the container you choose must have the following requirements:

Has Tightly-Closed Cap

It is required to have a cap that can tightly close and hold water when there are bumps and jumps. It should be made of durable, unbreakable materials; glass materials are futile in such situations, so those are not ideal. Use a container with a narrow opening so water can be poured out.

New Containers

It is highly prohibited to use containers that have been previously used to hold liquid or solid toxic chemicals, such as bleach and pesticides

Sanitize the Containers

It is recommended to clean and sanitize the water containers. Before filling your chosen containers with safe and clean water, use these steps to sanitize containers.

- Wash your chosen container and rinse it with water.
- Sanitize the container with a solution mixing one teaspoon of odorless liquid household chlorine bleach in one quart of water. Use bleach that contains 5 percent sodium hypochlorite.

- Close the container tightly with a cap and shake it well in all directions. Make sure the bleach solution touches all inside surfaces of the container.

- Wait at least 30 seconds, and then empty the sanitizing solution from the container.

- Let the empty container air-dry before use, or rinse the empty container with safe water.

- Can make it dry by putting containers in the open sun, which also disinfect the surface.

- Pour clean water into the container and cover with a tight lid.

Pouring Water

Precautions should be taken for removing safe water out of the container, otherwise you'll contaminate your container and the water. If using a scoop or pot, clean it before and after pouring out water from your container to avoid contamination of all the water. Be sure not to touch the container's water surface and walls with your hand or another thing while pouring water. Never pour out safe water using your hands.

Safety Tips

Tips for storing safe water in a container after cleaning and sanitizing:

- Label your container as "drinking water" and write the storage date. It will help remind you to change the water after a long time.
- Store your water in a place with a constant (50–70°F) cool temperature.
- Do not keep the water containers in direct sunlight.
- Do not keep the water containers in areas with toxic substances, such as gasoline or pesticides.
- Replace stored water every six months.

Water Purification Methods

Whether you are storing water for drinking or cooking purposes, the cleaner it is, the longer it will remain fresh. When you remove all the contaminants from the water, including microbes, it is likely to stay fresh for months. For this reason, different purifications are employed. Some of them can be tried at home or in any setting without the use of large-scale machines or equipment, and those methods include:

Boiling

It is the simplest of the purification methods and also a widely used one. In this method, the water is heated to its boiling point—the temperature at which most microbes cease to exist. Boiling must be employed to filter clean and soft water.

Water Purifier

Water can also be purified using an electric purifier. It has UV, UF, and carbon filters to remove all sorts of impurities from the water and provide you with the cleanest drinking water.

Reverse Osmosis

This method is a fairly popular one, and there are entire water plants that run to clean water through reverse osmosis. Not everyone can have this technology available at home, so you can simply buy water passed through an RO plant or let your stored water be processed through these plants. In this process, the water is passed through semipermeable membranes and then purified.

Water Chlorination

It is not a widely recommended technique, but it can be used to clean the water on an emergency basis. About 5 percent chlorine is added to the water, which then kills the microorganisms. This process is not recommended for drinking water.

Distillation

Distillation is rather a complex and complicated process, but it gives you the purest of water. It is not as effective as reverse osmosis because it removes all the minerals from the water along with the impurities. It is also time-consuming and cannot be carried out in home settings.

Solar Purification

The purification technique involves storing the water in food-grade plastic bottles, then shaking them well to activate the oxygen. Then, the bottles are kept in sunlight horizontally. By doing so, the viruses and bacteria are killed due to the UV rays.

Chapter 12

Making the Most of the Basics

Difficult times call for difficult measures; there are no regular means available to cook your food during emergencies and crises. So, you will need some simple and easy recipes that can be used to prepare basic meals without using a stove or a long list of ingredients. In this section, you will find some of the highly recommended survival food meal ideas that anyone can prepare using available cooking resources.

Hardtack

Since you can't bake complete bread during emergency times, the hardtack is a suitable option to go for. It requires basic ingredients which are usually stored in large amounts for survival purposes, and they include:

- 6 cups of flour
- 1 cup of water

These two ingredients are mixed together to prepare a dough, which is then cooked over hot rocks, on a griddle, or in a pan.

Pemmican

Pemmican is no-cook food that can be prepared easily in no time. It can offer many calories and energy, though, and that is why it is highly recommended on this list.

Pemmican is energy balls made out of lard, nuts, dried fruits, berries, and sometimes meat. The fat base is mixed with different ingredients for great taste and nutrition.

Jerky

Meat jerky is great for long-term storage, and is relatively easy to make. Use the following ingredients to make jerky.

- 2 pounds of boneless meat
- ½ cup soy sauce
- ¼ cup Worchester sauce
- ½ teaspoon of Morton Tender Quick Cure
- 1 teaspoon of chili powder
- 1 tablespoon of garlic powder
- 1 tablespoon of onion powder
- 2 tablespoons of cracked pepper

The meat is first sliced, then it is marinated using soy sauce, Worcestershire sauce, Morton Tender Quick Cure, garlic powder, and chili powder in a bowl. When the meat is marinated for four hours in the refrigerator or overnight, it can then be dehydrated in a dehydrator or the sunlight.

Biltong

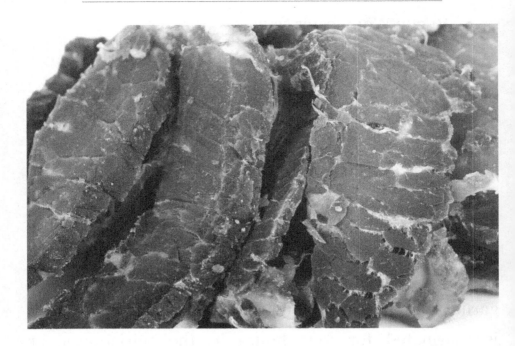

Like meat jerky, biltong is also prepared using the dehydrating method. However, the meat is seasoned and marinated with a different mixture of ingredients, including:

- 4 ½ pounds lean meat
- 2 cups brown sugar
- 3 cups plump sea salt
- 1 teaspoon baking soda
- 2 tablespoons black pepper
- 100 milliliters Worcestershire sauce
- 5 cups vinegar
- 4 tablespoons ground coriander seeds

The meat is mixed and marinated for four days and then dehydrated.

Dried Fruit

Dehydrated fruits are easy to store, and they are also a great source of energy. If you want to store them for a long time, then try home dehydration.

- Desired fruit
- ½ cup of lemon
- ½ cup of water

First, you will have to thinly slice the fruit, then soak its slices in the mixture of water and lemon juice. Place these slices either on a dehydrator plate to transfer to a dehydrator or dry them in the sunlight.

Beans and Rice

Rice and beans can be cooked in various ways, and that would only require some water, black pepper, salt, and the beans or the rice.

When you have these ingredients ready, first soak and rinse the dry beans or rice, then add them to a pot filled with water in double amount. Cook the beans for two hours at least until they are soft, and cook the rice for 30 minutes until they are tender. Now that you will have basic beans or rice meal, you can add other ingredients to make them more delicious, like a drizzle of stored cheese or some extra seasonings or herbs.

Ration Bars

These are the high-energy bars that are greatly recommended on this list. You can prepare them using stored items like:

- 6 cups oats
- 2 tablespoons chia seeds
- 3 tablespoons hemp flour or almond flour
- 2 tablespoons fruit powder
- 6 scoops protein powder
- 1 cup honey
- 1 cup coconut oil
- 12 tablespoons peanut butter

All these ingredients are mixed together in any container. It is best to blend them together if there is a blender available, or you can simply mix them using a spoon and then spread the mixture in a pan. The mixture hardens with time or on refrigeration. Cut the cake into bars and serve.

Snack Squares

- ½ cup peanut butter
- ½ cup honey
- 3 tablespoons margarine
- ½ cup instant nonfat dried milk
- 2 ½ cups cereal

Combine peanut butter, honey, and margarine in a saucepan. Stir over low heat until blended. Remove from heat. Stir in milk powder until well blended; mix in cereal. Press in an 8-inch square baking pan. Cool for one hour; cut into squares. Store in refrigerator.

Peanut Butter-Honey Balls

- ½ cup peanut butter
- ¼ cup honey
- ½–1 cup instant nonfat dried milk
- ½ cup cereal

Mix peanut butter and honey in a bowl; stir well. Slowly add milk powder; mix well. Add cereal to desired thickness; stir until mixed. Shape into small balls. Ready to eat! Store in refrigerator. Uncooked oatmeal, oat flakes, corn flakes, bran flakes, etc.

Spanish Wheat

- 3 strips bacon
- 1 medium onion, chopped
- 1 green pepper, diced
- 3 cups cooked whole wheat
- 2 ½ cups canned tomatoes
- Salt and black pepper, to taste

Cook bacon; remove from pan. Add onion and peppers, sauté until tender. Add wheat and tomatoes; cover and simmer for five hours. Top with crumbled bacon.

Mock Peanut Brittle

- ½ cup corn syrup
- ½ cup sugar
- ½ cup powdered milk
- 1 cup peanut butter
- 8 cups corn flakes

Combine corn syrup and sugar in a small saucepan. Over medium heat, stir to dissolve sugar. Add peanut butter and bring to boil. Remove from heat, add powdered milk, and mix well. Add corn flakes; put in the pan. Cool and cut into squares.

Whole Wheat Meat Loaf

- 1 ½ pounds ground beef
- 1 cup whole wheat, cooked
- 2 beaten eggs
- 1 cup milk
- ¼ cup onion, chopped
- 2 ½ teaspoons salt
- ¼ teaspoon pepper
- 1 teaspoon sage
- 1 teaspoon Worcestershire sauce
- 1 teaspoon prepared mustard

Combine all ingredients thoroughly and pack into a loaf pan. Top with sauce. Bake at 350 degrees for one hour.

Wheat and Bean Chili

- 1 cup uncooked dry beans
- 1 cup uncooked wheat
- 1 quart water
- 3 tablespoons fat
- 1 onion, chopped
- 1 pound ground beef
- 1 clove garlic
- 2 cups tomatoes
- 1 teaspoon chili powder
- Salt & paprika, to taste
- 2 teaspoons brown sugar
- ½ tablespoon catsup
- ½ teaspoon cumin seed

Cook beans and wheat together in one quart of water. Add more water if necessary. Cook until almost tender. Beans and wheat may be cooked in a pressure saucepan at 10 pounds pressure for 35 minutes after soaking. Sauté meat, onions, and garlic; drain. Combine meat mixture, beans, and rest of ingredients. Simmer for 1 hour.

Broccoli Wheat Bake

- 2 pounds broccoli, chopped
- ½ cup onion, chopped
- 1 tablespoon butter, melted
- 1 can cream of chicken soup
- ¼ cup dairy sour cream
- 1 cup grated carrot
- ½ cup milk
- 1 cup cheddar cheese, grated
- 2 cups cracked wheat, soaked

Sauté onion in butter; add soup and heat to boiling. Reduce heat and stir in remaining ingredients. Turn into a 2-quart casserole. Bake at about 350 degrees Fahrenheit for 30 minutes.

Wheat Fold-Overs

- 1 ½ cups whole wheat flour
- 1 teaspoon baking powder
- ¼ teaspoon salt
- ½ cup margarine or butter
- ½ cup brown sugar
- 1 egg
- 1 teaspoon vanilla

Cream butter; beat in sugar until fluffy. Add the vanilla and egg, then beat well. Add dry ingredients and blend well. Cover and chill for two hours. Roll dough to 1/8-inch thickness and cut in 2 ½-inch circles. Place 1 teaspoon filling at the center of each circle and fold in half; seal edges with a fork. Bake on a baking sheet at about 375 degrees Fahrenheit for 12 minutes; cool on a rack. Drizzle with icing.

Hot Chocolate Mix

- ½ pound instant chocolate drink
- 5 cups instant powdered milk
- ¾ cup nondairy creamer
- ¼ cup powdered sugar

Mix together. Stir 1/3 cup of mix into 1 cup hot water.

Hot Chocolate Mix II

- 2 cups sugar
- 2 ½ cups instant powdered milk
- ¾ cup cocoa
- 1 ½ cups creamer

Mix together. Stir 2 tablespoons of mix into ¾ to 1 cup of hot water.

Sweetened Condensed Milk

- 2 cups dry powdered milk
- 1 cup hot tap water
- 2 cups sugar
- 2 tablespoons butter

Put milk and water into the blender; mix well. Add sugar and butter and blend well; refrigerate.

Peanut Butter Chews

- ½ cup peanut butter
- ½ cup corn syrup
- ½ cup powdered sugar
- 1 cup dry milk

Mix peanut butter with corn syrup and gradually add powdered sugar. Mix well until smooth. Then add dry milk a little at a time and mix well until the mixture is stiff enough to handle. Then roll into your choice of shapes.

Buttermilk

- ½ cup buttermilk
- 3 cups warm water
- 1 cup nonfat dry milk
- 1 ½ cups instant nonfat dry milk

Put buttermilk, water, and dry milk in a large clean jar and stir or shake until milk is dissolved. Cover this jar with a lid or clean cloth. Let stand in a warm room until mixture clabbers (about 10 hours in the winter or five hours in the summer). After it clabbers, store in the refrigerator.

White Sauce Mix

- 2 cups instant nonfat dry milk
- 1 ½ cups regular nonfat dry milk
- 1 cup all-purpose flour
- 1 cup butter
- 2 teaspoons salt

In a suitable bowl, mix dry milk, flour, and salt; mix well. Cut in butter until the mixture looks like fine crumbs. Store in an airtight container in the refrigerator. Use within two months.

Corn Chowder

- 5 bacon slices
- 1 medium onion, sliced
- 2 medium potatoes, pared and diced
- Water
- 1 teaspoon salt, black pepper
- 2 cups milk
- 17 ounces can cream corn
- 1 cup above white sauce mix
- 1 tablespoon butter or margarine

In a frying pan, cook bacon until crispy. Crumble and set aside. Reserve 3 tablespoons of bacon drippings in the pan. Stir in onion and cook until light brown. Add potatoes and enough water to cover. Cook over medium heat 10–15 minutes until potatoes are cooked. Combine milk and white sauce mix in a small saucepan. Then cook on low heat until thick and smooth. Stir in corn, salt, and black pepper. Toss in potato mixture and heat through about 10 minutes. Top with crumbled bacon and butter.

Tomato Soup

- 4 cups crushed tomatoes
- ¼ cup onion, chopped
- 1 bay leaf
- ½ teaspoon basic, crushed dried
- Salt and black pepper, to taste
- 2 cups milk
- ½ cup white sauce mix

In a saucepan, combine the first five ingredients. Simmer 5 minutes; remove bay leaf. In another saucepan, combine milk and white sauce mix; thicken over medium heat. Slowly add hot tomato mixture to white sauce, stirring constantly. Serve immediately.

Pudding Mix

- 1 ½ cups sugar
- 2 ½ cups nonfat dry milk
- 1 teaspoon salt
- ¾ cup cornstarch

Mix all ingredients together, store in a tightly covered container in a cool place.

Cream Soup Mix

- 2 cups powdered nonfat milk
- ¾ cup cornstarch
- ¼ cup instant chicken bouillon
- 2 tablespoons dried onion flakes
- 1 teaspoon basil leaves
- 1 teaspoon thyme leaves
- ½ teaspoon black pepper

Combine all ingredients, mixing well. Store in an airtight container until ready to use.

Yogurt

- 2 cups warm water
- 1 cup non-instant powdered milk
- 2 tablespoons plain yogurt

Pour warm water into a blender. Add milk and blend well. Add yogurt and blend. Pour into jars or glasses. Place jars neck-deep in warm water. Cover with a lid. Maintain temperature 100–120 degrees for 3–4 hours. The mixture should clabber or set up. Chill immediately. Sweeten to taste; use in dips, dressings, in place of sour cream. It may also be used in desserts.

Conclusion

Did you find all that information useful? Are you going to manage and organize your pantry using all the tips shared in this comprehensive guide? Well, then it will definitely make the tedious and exhausting process of long-term food storage easy and simple enough to understand! There are many different aspects of stockpiling, and all of those are thoroughly discussed in different chapters of this stockpiling guide. It will not only teach you to stock your pantry, but it will also leave you with the complete idea of managing and maintaining a pantry according to your needs and using the right types of tools and equipment. Use each chapter as a reference. You move from one step to the second. And see how simple it can get, all because of the right guidance and proper planning!

Made in the USA
Monee, IL
13 October 2024